I0737523

Living Hope

Scriptures & Reflections
to Increase Your Faith

warnerpress

30580PO100000041

Warner Press, Inc.
Warner Press and Warner Press logo are trademarks of Warner Press, Inc.

Edited by: Julie Campbell
Cover and Layout by: Curtis Corzine

Hebrews 11:1 (KJV)

Faith is the substance of things hoped for, the evidence of things not seen.

Have you ever read Hebrews 11, aka "The Faith Chapter," and marveled at the faith of the people listed there? It's like taking a walk through the Saints' Hall of Fame—Abel, Enoch, Noah, Abraham, Sarah, Isaac, Rahab, Jacob, Moses, and many more. They were all seemingly ordinary people who did amazing things for God. *I could never measure up*, you might think. But here's some good news: Their hope is the same hope you have today. Their God is the same God you serve today. Their faith is the same faith you possess today. Living by faith and having hope in God's promises aren't just for the saints of Bible times; they're for you too. As a Christ follower, you are part of the larger tapestry of faith, weaving throughout history as part of God's plan. Someday that glorious plan will be complete, the picture will become crystal clear, and our faith will become sight.

Julie Campbell

Ephesians 2:8 (NIV)

*It is by grace you have been saved,
through faith—and this is not from yourselves,
it is the gift of God.*

Faith is the wire
that connects
you to grace,
and over which
grace comes
streaming from God.

Unknown

Psalm 86:11 (NIV)

Teach me your way, LORD, that I may rely on your faithfulness.

Have you ever seen photos of people who look like their pets? A girl has a hairdo like her sheepdog. A man has a beard like his Schnauzer. How about the ones of husbands and wives who look alike? Some of those are so funny! But they point out an important fact: We become like the ones we spend the most time with. To really know someone takes effort. If all goes well, we grow in our understanding and build a strong relationship.

Developing a relationship with Jesus works in much the same way. To know Jesus better, I must spend time communicating with Him in prayer. I discover His likes and dislikes as I read the Bible. I create a philosophy of life grounded in His truth and founded on my faith in Him. My hope is that the more time I spend with Jesus, the more I will look like Him.

Robin Loisch

Psalm 90:1-2 (NIV)

Lord, you have been our dwelling place throughout all generations.... From everlasting to everlasting you are God.

O God, our help
in ages past,
Our hope for years
to come,
Our shelter from the
stormy blast,
And our eternal home!

Isaac Watts

Revelation 3:20 (NIV)

Here I am! I stand at the door and knock.

When I was a teenager, I was a student leader for both my church youth group and the Campus Life group at my high school. I really enjoyed these roles, but I often found myself volunteering and striving to the point of burn out. I ended up feeling tired and unfulfilled in my relationship with Christ. When I talked about what I was feeling with my youth leader, he said to me, "Being busy isn't going to bring you closer to God. Slow down and open your heart to Him."

My gut instinct is to make everything into a goal, something to be accomplished, and then work hard to accomplish it. And while it's important to serve and to use our gifts to further God's kingdom and spread the gospel, those things aren't going to bring us any closer to God. He's *already* close. He's waiting on us to open our hearts to Him. We don't have to seek and strive; all we have to do is open the door.

Elizabeth Flinn

Lamentations 3:25 (NIV)

The LORD is good to those whose hope is in him,
to the one who seeks him.

Life with Christ
is an endless hope,
without Him
a hopeless end.

Unknown

Psalm 33:20 (NIV)

We wait in hope for the LORD; he is our help and our shield.

Just like our health grows better as we exercise, hope grows as it is exercised. How do I exercise hope? What do I do with hope? Hope is a confident expectation that God, who has begun a good work already, will complete this good work. Because hope is a part of the Good News, I know what I am supposed to do with the Good News. The song *Pass It On* says: "That's how it is with God's love once you've experienced it. You spread his love to everyone." Hope is part of the love. When we receive God's grace, we receive a new heart and right spirit. We also contribute to the growth of hope—in ourselves and others. Hope, which is a gift of God, is something I can pass along.

Drexel Rankin

Psalm 31:14–15 (NIV)

But I trust in you, LORD; I say, "You are my God."
My times are in your hands.

Whether I live or die,
Whether I wake or sleep,
Whether upon the land
Or on the stormy deep;
When 'tis serene
and calm
Or when the wild
winds blow,
I shall not be afraid—
I am the Lord's, I know.

Charles W. Naylor

Isaiah 26:3 (NLT)

*You will keep in perfect peace
all who trust in you.*

Clashes in politics, constant changes in the economy, a crumbling moral foundation—no wonder we struggle to stand upright at times, when both our environment and our own emotions crash down on us so often. Yet even in this turbulence, we can trust that our God will never change. Because God remains the same, we can trust Him completely. When we place our confidence in the Lord instead of focusing on the changes around us or even within us, we can find unparalleled peace. Today, instead of focusing on our inadequacies, let's focus on our sufficient God. Thank Him for His unchanging nature and for His promise of perfect peace. Let your thoughts relax as you allow Him to be your steadfast hope in a turbulent world.

Stephanie Hansen

Jeremiah 29:11 (NIV)

"For I know the plans I have for you," declares the Lord, "plans to...give you hope and a future."

Hope is daring to imagine that life is the way you envision it to be, and faith makes that hope a reality.

Cheryl Smith

1 Peter 5:7 (NIV)

Cast all your anxiety on him because he cares for you.

The sun streamed through the windowpane at just the right angle to cast the shadow of a cross on the opposite wall. As the sun rose, the cross faded, then disappeared. Even though I start each day focused on Scripture reading and prayer, laying my burdens at the foot of the cross, many times as the day progresses, I pick those cares and burdens up again, and the power of the cross fades away just as quickly as that shadow. We magnify what we focus on, so when we concentrate on our cares and concerns, the power of the cross diminishes. Peace fades quickly when we consume ourselves with our troubles. Lord, help us to be aware of Your presence and power throughout our day, inviting You into every care that concerns us, that You may be magnified, and that we may live in Your hope and peace.

Jane Glenchur

Proverbs 3:6 (NLT)

Seek his will in all you do, and he will show you which path to take.

The journey of life takes us on many different roads.

Some are straight, some winding, some smooth, some bumpy.

You may not know what lies ahead, but rest assured—God knows and He promises never to leave you.

Karen Rhodes

Isaiah 41:10 (NIV)

Do not fear, for I am with you....
I will strengthen you and help you.

When I was a teen, I went on a cave exploration trip with my youth group. Crawling around with flashlights in a cave was exhilarating at first, but some recent rains had transformed the cave floor into a slippery mess. At one point, we had to climb up a steep incline to get to a new level in the cave. As I was almost to the top, my feet started slipping and my hands had nothing to grab but mud. Just when I thought I couldn't hang on any longer, my older brother heard my cries for help, held out his hand, and pulled me up with his strong grasp. The relief I felt was overwhelming!

A similar scenario often plays out in my daily life. Just when I'm at my weakest and ready to give up, Jesus offers me His gentle, helping hand. He looks at me with loving, not scolding, eyes and says, "I'm here, child. I know what you're going through, and I'm going to help you."

Julie Campbell

Micah 7:7 (NIV)

But as for me, I watch in hope for the LORD,
I wait for God my Savior.

Waiting teaches us patience.

As we wait on the Lord,
we learn life-lessons about
what it really means to trust.

Our faith is tested and proven
strong and sure.

We discover that Jesus
is the true source of our
hope and peace.

And when Jesus is all that
we have, we realize that
Jesus is all that we need.

Robin Loisch

Galatians 4:6 (NIV)

God sent the Spirit of his Son into our hearts, the Spirit who calls out, "Abba, Father."

Several years ago, my father and I hiked a mountain. We had done many hikes before, but this was the toughest one we had ever attempted. We planned to reach the summit and return to the parking lot before dark, so we took little food and only light jackets. We were on the trail at sunup and thought we would have had plenty of time, but the steep terrain slowed us down and we ran out of daylight—still miles away from the car and without flashlights. As the sun vanished over the horizon and we stood there in the dark, I called out to my father in fear: "What are we going to do? We've got to keep going!" But my father knew that there were some other hikers behind us who likely had flashlights. He encouraged me to wait, and within an hour these hikers caught up to us and we walked the rest of the way out with them. By God's Spirit in our hearts, we can cry out to God in our darkest times. Our heavenly Father will bring the light we need to move ahead.

Kevin Stiffler

Deuteronomy 31:8 (NLT)

Do not be afraid or discouraged, for the LORD will personally go ahead of you.

Hope is a thousand
stars to light the
darkened night,
a candle burning
across eternity.

Hope is Jesus holding
you so near you can
hear His heartbeat.

Hope on!

Linda E. Knight

Psalm 23:1 (NLT)

The Lord is my shepherd; I have all that I need.

You may have heard someone described as "the black sheep of the family." Or maybe you are more familiar with an "ugly duckling," "lone wolf," or "horse of a different color." The English language is filled with animal descriptors for people who don't fit in with the crowd for one reason or another.

Perhaps you feel that person is you.

The good news is that Jesus does not view you that way. Today, Jesus wants you to know you belong. Young or old, rich or poor, healthy or sick, we all are invited by the Good Shepherd to become a part of His flock. Jesus doesn't require perfection; He wants us to come just as we are.

Robin Loisch

Psalm 27:5 (NIV)

In the day of trouble he will keep me safe in his dwelling.

When answers fail
and dreams fade,
where can we go
but to Jesus?

He whispers peace,
and like a child we run
to His open arms.

Rebecca Barlow Jordan

Matthew 5:16 (NIV)

Let your light shine before others, that they may... glorify your Father in heaven.

The soaring walls of my childhood church were punctuated with glorious stained-glass windows. One week, our Sunday school teacher gave us a special tour of the windows. She taught us how the artist used colored glass and design to tell the stories of Jesus—not just to us, but to the world. You see, when we were sitting in the pews and the sun was shining outside, our congregation could see the images. But when the lights were turned on inside the church, everyone in our community could see the beautiful windows too! It was a way of sharing the life of Jesus with the whole neighborhood. It's not that different with our own lives. God's light shines into our hearts, but when we let that same light shine out of us, we let the whole world see the gospel living in us. In that moment, God's glory illuminates our lives, our works, and our love, and everything points to Jesus!

Allison Lynn

Hebrews 13:8 (NIV)

Jesus Christ is the same yesterday
and today and forever.

Let nothing
disturb thee,
Let nothing
affright thee,
All things
are passing,
God changeth never.

Henry Wadsworth Longfellow

Psalm 32:8 (NIV)

I will instruct you and teach you in the way you should go.

One sunny day, I was driving down a country road when out of nowhere, I saw something shocking. Cows. I live in the country, so seeing cows shouldn't be that surprising. But these particular cows were standing on the side of the road, roaming free! When they saw me in my SUV, they looked a bit surprised as well. As I made my turn onto the next country road, they followed me! When I pulled into the driveway of the farmhouse where they belonged, they ran right up to the gate of the pasture. Those cows needed some serious direction. And you know what? So do I. There are times in my life when I feel like those scared, directionless cows. Lost. Alone. And yet, instead of praying and asking the One who promises me direction, what do I do? I fret. I worry. I try to fix things myself. James 1:5 (NIV) says, *If any of you lacks wisdom, you should ask God.* The God of the Universe is willing to offer His wisdom and direction to us—all we have to do is ask!

Julie Campbell

Jeremiah 17:7 (NIV)

Blessed is the one who trusts in the Lord,
whose confidence is in him.

Every tomorrow
has two handles.
We can take hold
of it with the handle
of anxiety or
the handle
of faith.

Henry Ward Beecher

John 14:27 (NIV)

Peace I leave with you; my peace I give you....
Do not let your hearts be troubled.

I always know my life has gotten too busy when I can no longer find my peace. Yes, adorning my nightstand, I literally have a wooden cut-out of the letters P-E-A-C-E. The only other items that are *supposed* to share this space are a Bible, a book light, and my reading glasses. But too often, additional things crowd the surface—my phone, a novel, sticky notes, pens, and pencils. Soon the Bible is covered up. And my P-E-A-C-E? It's gone, fallen, lying upside-down on the floor. It is no coincidence that my life at these moments often erupts with impatience, a lack of compassion, and fears about tomorrow. I must find peace. What a loving God we have. Even though we make our lives messy and neglect responding to Him, He welcomes us back. He offers us rest, contentment, and forgiveness time and again in His Word.

Miriam Lunz

Isaiah 43:2 (NIV)

*When you pass through the waters,
I will be with you.*

The One who made both the tiny stream and the raging current holds you in the palm of His hand, and you are safe—no matter what is swirling all around you.

Isaiah 35:1–2 (NIV)

The wilderness will rejoice and blossom.
Like the crocus, it will burst into bloom.

The garden at our new home had been ignored for years. Tall weeds choked out everything. The soil was dust. I grabbed my pruners and trowel but soon realized nothing had survived under the brambly mess. I would need to start from scratch the following spring. But as the weather warmed, little tips of green pushed through the soil. I eyed them expectantly. Almost overnight, the front yard was a carpet of crocuses! Their little stems stood at attention, topped with nodding purple heads. These delicate beauties had been smothered by strangling weeds, but with a little love and sunshine, they came back to life. We're not that different. Worries and doubts can smother us. We need to create space for the nourishment of living water and the warmth of God's loving light. What are the things we need to prune and clear away so we can grow in hope and live life to the fullest?

Allison Lynn

Hebrews 6:19 (NIV)

We have this hope as an anchor for the soul, firm and secure.

Faith is a living and unshakable confidence, a belief in the grace of God so assured that a man would die a thousand deaths for its sake.

Martin Luther

1 Thessalonians 5:16–18 (NIV)

Rejoice always, pray continually, give thanks in all circumstances.

What would you do if someone told you there were nine words that, if you applied them, would change your life? You'd want to know right away where you could find those words, wouldn't you? You might even pay money to read a book or a blog post on the topic! Not surprisingly, those nine simple words are right in the Bible. You've probably read them before, maybe you've even memorized them at some point in your life. 1 Thessalonians 5:16–18 (NIV): *Rejoice always, pray continually, give thanks in all circumstances.* Nine simple words, but not so simple to apply daily! The verse goes on to say that these nine words wrap up God's will for you in a nutshell! So, today, why not commit these nine words to memory? By rejoicing always, praying continually, and giving thanks in all circumstances, you'll not only find peace and contentment, but you'll also be doing God's will for your life.

Julie Campbell

Romans 15:13 (KJV)

Now the God of hope fill you with all joy and peace in believing.

Hope opens doors where despair closes them.

Hope discovers what can be done instead of grumbling about what cannot be done.

Hope draws its power from a deep trust in God.

Daniel 2:22 (NIV)

He reveals deep and hidden things; he knows what lies in darkness, and light dwells with him.

When I was a dermatologist, I loved looking through my microscope at skin biopsies and seeing exactly what was causing the rash or growth on my patient's skin. What was not obvious to my unaided eyes became clear under magnification. Seeing such tiny details at the cellular level cleared up the mystery of why the patient might not be responding to treatment or might need a different remedy. Whenever I pray, it comforts me greatly to be reminded that God sees every detail of my concerns, whether it is a family member's illness, a misunderstanding, or a difficult decision that needs to be made. God sees the big picture but also those hidden things we cannot see with human eyes. Nothing escapes His attention. Nothing is hidden from Him.

Jane Glenchur

Psalm 42:5 (NIV)

Put your hope in God, for I will yet praise him.

Once a saint puts
his confidence
in...God,
no tribulation
or affliction
can ever touch
that confidence.

Oswald Chambers

Habakkuk 3:17–18 (NIV)

Though the fig tree does not bud and there are no grapes on the vines,... yet I will rejoice in the Lord.

I had never seen a wild blackberry here before. For over a month I had walked this same path on my college campus, drinking in the beauty of God's creation as I lifted my hungry soul for Him to fill. My heart still ached from the loss of my best friend. But this time, as I prayed for God's presence, I discovered something new. Half hidden within the bushes lining the path, a single scarlet berry gleamed up at me—hope in the wilderness. Often, when we experience trials, we cannot sense the Lord at work in our lives.

Unlike most fruits, fig blossoms grow *inside* the fruit. Because of this unusual growth, one never sees the blossom itself, even when it is there. Although we might not see God's work blossoming within our lives, we can rejoice that He is always growing our faith in Him. As we faithfully seek Him in the wilderness, He will reveal the fruit from our reliance on Him.

Stephanie Hansen

Philippians 4:7 (NIV)

The peace of God, which transcends all understanding, will guard your hearts and your minds in Christ Jesus.

When peace, like a river
attendeth my way,
When sorrows like
sea billows roll—
Whatever my lot,
Thou hast taught
me to say,
It is well, it is well
with my soul.

Horatio G. Spafford

Proverbs 5:21 (NIV)

Your ways are in full view of the Lord,
and he examines all your paths.

In my work as a pet sitter, I routinely enter client homes to care for their animals, usually while the owners are away at work or traveling. Twenty-first century homes often have cameras inside and out, so I have been taught to assume I am being watched while working and to always behave accordingly. I'm aware the pet parents may laugh at my baby talk and silly songs, but hopefully they also see the love and care I show their pets. God, on the other hand, doesn't need cameras to see us. Ever omnipotent, He watches everything we do. That may sound scary, having all our sins on display, so we should definitely try to act like the Christians we are. But God's attentive eye also notices when we do good and care for others, and I imagine that makes God smile. Plus, God can see when we need help, and He supports us through the problem. We are always watched by the loving gaze of our greatest ally.

Kim Sheard

Psalm 71:14 (KJV)

I will hope continually, and will yet praise thee more and more.

Behind the cloud
the starlight lurks,
Through showers
the sunbeams fall;
For God, who loveth
all His works,
Has left His hope for all.

John Greenleaf Whittier

Numbers 6:25 (NIV)

The Lord make his face shine on you and be gracious to you.

"You have the countenance of Christ." My friend's words caught me off guard. I had never imagined possessing Christ's countenance. In fact, I had been so wrapped up in feelings of insufficiency that I didn't even think my heart resembled Christ, even if the smile on my face did. Often revisiting that memory, I have come to recognize a deep sense of peace that settles over my heart when I spend time with certain people—special friends who just seem to radiate Christ's presence. Their quietness of spirit eases the tension within my own. This truth reminds me of God's blessing on the nation of Israel in Numbers 6:24–26. God blessed the Israelites not only with His favor but also with the special hope of His peace. As believers, we have that hope in Christ. May we lead others to this same bright hope by reflecting Christ in our lives.

Stephanie Hansen

Psalm 33:18 (NIV)

The eyes of the LORD are on those…whose hope is in his unfailing love.

Hope writes the poetry
of the boy,
but memory that
of the man.

Man looks forward
with smiles,
but backward with sighs.

Such is the wise
providence of God.

The cup of life is sweetest
at the brim.

Adolphe Monod

Philippians 4:13 (NIV)

I can do all this through him who gives me strength.

It was hopeless! All the clutter in my bedroom had defeated me for years. Every inch of my corner desk was smothered in books, articles, and to-do lists. The drawers ached from being overstuffed. Perfectionism stopped me cold in my tracks. Tackling the clutter was impossible, so why try? Then one day I read that you cannot conquer procrastination by waiting to *feel* motivated. The solution is simple: Just do *one* thing. Motivation will *follow*. I asked the Holy Spirit for wisdom—what to keep, what to pitch, and what to give away. Then I opened my messiest drawer, took out one item, and tossed it. That one step motivated me to discard half the contents and organize the rest. Victory! Is procrastination paralyzing you? Are you putting off praying or reading Scripture? Try reading one verse or praying for one family member. You might be surprised how that will jump start your spiritual life. If your spiritual life is cluttered, you now hold the key to getting unstuck. Just do one thing!

Jane Glenchur

James 1:17 (KJV)

Every good gift and every perfect gift
is from above.

In all the ranks of life
the human heart yearns
for the beautiful;
and the beautiful things
that God makes
are his gift to all alike.

Harriet Beecher Stowe

James 4:8 (NIV)

Come near to God and he will come near to you.

If you've ever shopped for a house, you've probably heard the phrase "location, location, location." The repetition of the word "location" emphasizes the importance of *where* a house is situated and how its value increases, or decreases, based on its location. The Bible has a lot to say about our location as well. If you're a believer, you're protected by God in many ways. Psalm 91:4 (NIV) uses the imagery of a mother bird protecting her young: *He will cover you with his feathers, and under his wings you will find refuge*. But even when we're sinking in our sin or suffering the consequences of bad choices, God can change our location. *He lifted me out of the slimy pit, out of the mud and mire; he set my feet on a rock and gave me a firm place to stand* (Psalm 40:2 NIV) Thank God today for His nearness to you and for making your heart His home!

Julie Campbell

Psalm 147:11 (NIV)

The Lord delights in those who fear him,
who put their hope in his unfailing love.

My hope is built on
nothing less
Than Jesus' blood
and righteousness;
I dare not trust the
sweetest frame,
But wholly lean
on Jesus' name.

Edward Mote

Romans 5:5 (NLT)

This hope will not lead to disappointment. For we know how dearly God loves us.

Someone must ask the question, and John the Baptist does. What seems certain in sunlight often loses its certainty in shadows. An imprisoned John asks: *Are you the one who is to come, or should we expect someone else?* (Luke 7:19 NIV) Doubts come easily to people in trying circumstances. This world where we live changes and twirls all around us. Economically and politically, many foundations on which we have based our hopes may have crashed. We realize that we must look for another hope, not one based on material possessions. What is reality today may not be here tomorrow—no matter how desperately we want it. We seek a lifestyle that says: "Despite the shadows, I know that the Spirit of Christ is upon me. It blossoms in my life. I know His hope for me and for the world. Let me show it to you by my living."

Drexel Rankin

John 16:32 (KJV)

I am not alone, because the Father is with me.

"A still small voice"
comes through the wild,
Like a father consoling
his fretful child,
Which banishes
bitterness, wrath,
and fear,
Saying—Man is distant,
but God is near!

Thomas Pringle

Philippians 4:19 (KJV)

My God shall supply all your need according to his riches in glory by Christ Jesus.

The little red arrow was inching nearer to that dreaded E. I knew we should have filled up after lunch. As the tank got closer to empty, my anxiety got closer to overflow. Suddenly, a tall sign reached above the trees. A gas station was one exit away! I prayed the drops in the bottom of our tank would be enough. Just as the red arrow finally touched the E, I pulled up to the pump and turned off the car. We'd made it. How many times are we like this in our spiritual lives? We plow through life, thinking we can make it on our own. We ignore the warning signs that our fuel is getting low and then wonder why we're struggling. But unlike our close call on the highway, we don't need to hunt for a gas station. Our Source is always close at hand, ready to fill us with strength, hope, and peace. God's supply is unlimited and always exactly what we need.

Allison Lynn

Psalm 55:22 (NIV)

Cast your cares on the LORD and he will sustain you.

Hope is like
the sun, which,
as we journey
toward it,
casts the shadow
of our
burden behind.

Samuel Smiles

John 8:12 (NIV)

I am the light of the world. Whoever follows me will never walk in darkness.

As an amateur photographer, I often find myself on a treasure hunt, chasing vibrant rainbows or pastel sunsets with my camera in hand. Other times, I'm taking candid shots of family members to document a birthday or wedding. But no matter the occasion, one element makes the best photo—lighting. For outdoor photos, natural light is always best, especially at the "golden hour," which is a photographer's term for the first hour after sunrise or the last hour before sunset. The world is bathed in a golden glow that makes every subject a little more luminous and magical.

Far better than the golden hour, the light of Jesus transforms us in ways natural lighting cannot. When our hearts are illuminated by His light, we are changed forever. He erases the shadows from our lives and fills them with His love, joy, and peace—not just for a split-second snapshot, but for all eternity.

Julie Campbell

Philippians 3:20 (NIV)

Our citizenship is in heaven. And we eagerly await a Savior from there, the Lord Jesus Christ.

I know on Whom my
faith is fixed,
I know in Whom I trust;
I know that Christ
abides in me,
And all His ways
are just.

Charles W. Naylor

Please e-mail the authors your comments and personal *What Would You Do If* experiences and payoffs at WhatwouldUdoif1@cs.com.

working with persons with disabilities. She loves being a stay-at-home mom and views each day as an adventure. She and her family currently reside in South Jordan, Utah.

Kim Osborne is the mother of two children. She is a stay-at-home mom who finds joy in the everyday craziness of motherhood. She holds various leadership positions serving children within her community. She has worked in various management and product marketing positions with a prominent retail company. She has a love for travel and enjoys exploring Europe with her husband. Her family currently resides in Draper, Utah.

About the Authors

Kim Osborne and Shalmarie Bunker

Shalmarie Bunker is the mother of three children. She has a Bachelor's Degree in English as well as a Secondary Education Degree, both from the University of Utah. She has worked extensively in educational, day treatment and recreational settings with children. She has spent a great deal of time